THE ULTIMATE BOOK OF SONG STARTERS

---

501 Powerful and Creative Ideas for Writing New Songs

ED BELL

Bell, Ed
Book : The Ultimate Book of Song Starters: 501 Powerful and Creative Ideas for Writing New Songs

Library of Congress Control Number: 2019910731

ISBN 978-1-7333750-2-3 (Paperback)
ISBN 978-1-7333750-3-0 (eBook)

First published August 2019
New York City

THE ULTIMATE BOOK OF SONG STARTERS:
501 POWERFUL AND CREATIVE IDEAS
FOR WRITING NEW SONGS

CONTENTS

Ready: How to Use This Book ix

Set: How to Use Each Starter Type xv

Write: The 501 Song Starters 1

Coda: Fear of the Blank Page – and How to Get Over It 257

Appendix: Chord Symbols Quick Guide 261

ABOUT THE SONG FOUNDRY

At The Song Foundry it's our mission to share great songwriting ideas with the world. At thesongfoundry.com we publish articles about songwriting, host free videos on various songwriting topics, and offer Skype songwriting coaching worldwide.

Connect with us online to find out more:

thesongfoundry.com

youtube.com/TheSongFoundry

facebook.com/TheSongFoundry

twitter.com/TheSongFoundry

[READY]
HOW TO USE THIS BOOK

'What if?' might just be the two most powerful words in the English language. They're the start of something new. They're the first spark of inspiration. They're the catalyst that starts the chain reaction that leads to a new 'what if?' and a new 'what if?' and a new 'what if?' after that.

And, well, if you're a songwriter looking for 501 powerful, interesting and creative ways to ask yourself 'what if?', you've come to the right place.

Now, truth be told, you don't really need this book. There are thousands of great song ideas all around you just waiting for you to notice them. They're in the songs you're listening to already. They're out on the street. They're in the news. And they're in the conversations – good, bad and ugly – you're having with the most important people in your life.

But hold on – don't throw this book out just yet. While you might not 100% need a book like this, you can absolutely, 100% use a book like this – and it might just help you create something you'd never have thought of on your own.

So if you're new to songwriting and you're looking for some inspiring but tried-and-tested song ideas to get you started, or you're the kind of songwriter who needs an extra push taking that first bold step on a song, or you're just excited to push your songwriting in a completely new direction, that's exactly what this book is going to give you, 501 times over.

So here we are – welcome to the ultimate collection of 501 different ideas, concepts and starting points you could use to spark literally thousands of songs.

The 501 song prompts fit into five basic types. Some give you a song concept, situation or story to write with. Some give you a single word or phrase. Some give you a chord progression of four or sometimes eight measures. Some give you a specific rhythm. And some of the most interesting ones give you more individual and even unusual ways to approach writing new songs.

I've tried to keep the song starters as simple as possible. Some are as short as a single word, and the longest are only two or three sentences. I didn't want to include tons of instructions or even guidance with each prompt because – like I do in most of my books – I'd rather plant some powerful ideas in your mind, then let you have fun figuring out how to use that idea in your own way. (Because, honestly, that's the best way to write songs and the best way to have fun while you do.)

So instead, before we get to the song starters, I'm going to give you some general pointers on working with each of the five types, if you find that sort of thing useful. If you are looking for some specific guidance on how to create new songs out of nothing, there's plenty more of that in my book *How to Write a Song (Even If You've Never Written One Before and You Think You Suck)*, which will be the ideal companion to this one.

If you're looking for a more structured way to try out tons of interesting songwriting techniques and ideas, you'll probably also enjoy my 30-Day Songwriting Challenges – especially *The 30-Day Speed Songwriting Challenge*, which will guide you through finishing fifteen brand new songs in a single month. There's more information about all of these books at the back of this one or on The Song Foundry website.

The starters in this book are organized pretty much at random – though a few of them with related themes or ideas are on nearby pages – so you can jump in and start working on whatever ideas inspire you most. Some of the starters were inspired by or cribbed from well-known or even crazily popular songs, but a) I'm not going to tell you which, and b) it doesn't really matter anyway, because a good idea is a good idea, wherever it comes from.

On that note, some of the starters will work great if you're interested in writing commercial pop music, and some not so much. But that's true whatever your goals are as a songwriter: some of these starters will be perfect for you, some you might want to pass on, and the rest will be somewhere in between. That's why you've got five hundred of them – and why I'm going to leave it to you to pick out the ones that inspire you most so you can make something cool with them.

It probably goes without saying that you can – actually, should – use them to write songs in any style or genre you like, with any combination of instruments, tracks and/or singers you like. All I've done with this book is put 501 simple but powerful song ideas painstakingly together in one place – ideas that are inspiring, stimulating and really well suited to writing, singing and/or making music about in virtually any genre. All so this book can become your songwriting bible any time you're feeling stuck or short of inspiration, or just feel like writing something that's an exciting new challenge for you.

So dive in. See what sparks your imagination. Pick out a 'what if?' or five hundred and see where they take you.

Happy writing.

A QUICK WORD ON COPYRIGHT

(Because some of y'all often ask.)

So here's the deal with copyright: in general, **you can't copyright an idea.**

Song ideas, song titles, chord progressions, the key of G major, the idea that the word 'party' should be pronounced 'pardy' – none of those things are copyrightable on their own. Copyright applies only to a specific *expression* or *use* of an idea, not a vague or general idea in itself.

So if you use any of the song starters in this book to write a megahit that makes you a gajillion dollars, don't expect me to write to you demanding a cut. Because I won't, because I can't. (Though you're welcome to email me to say thanks, if you like. I'd love that.)

But seriously for a second, copyright *does* matter any time you take material directly from existing in-copyright songs, as a few of the starters in this book suggest you do.

If it's just a title, a chord progression or the general idea of a song, that's fine – there's no copyright in any of those things. If you're writing just for yourself, you can do what you like there too. But if you directly quote or sample material from a song that's under copyright and want to distribute and/or make money from your new song, you'll need to get prior permission from whoever owns the copyright to the original song or songs you used.

Obviously I'm not an attorney so this definitely isn't official legal advice, yada, yada, yada. If you want further clarification on any of this, you should consult a qualified legal professional.

[SET]

HOW TO USE EACH STARTER TYPE

You know the drill: this is your book – you own it, so you can do whatever you like with it.

But in case it helps, let's spend a moment talking about the five different types of song starters you'll find in this book and what you can do to turn each of them into complete songs.

If you don't need any of this, and want to jump ahead and get writing, that's great. Go ahead. But if you're looking for some gentle pointers, there definitely are a handful of things that are worth knowing about each starter type. (And again, if you want some less gentle pointers, you'll probably find my book *How to Write a Song (Even If You've Never Written One Before and You Think You Suck)* perfect for that.)

Obviously, there's no single, 'correct' way to write a song – that's one of the reasons songwriting is so interesting and so rewarding. But by dividing these starters into five categories it not only made it easier for me to come up with 501 of them, it probably also makes it easier for you to get into a bit of a groove when it comes to working with them. (Pun, I guess, totally intended.)

So let's talk about the five types.

IDEA STARTERS

Idea starters are some of the most powerful and interesting starters in the book. They give you the classic song prompt-style starters like 'Write a song that says X' or 'Write a song from Y person to Z person' or 'Write a song that tells the story of person W, Ñ or Ö'.

They look like this:

Write a song that says 'You're the best thing that's ever happened to me.'

Use this idea, situation or concept to build a complete song.

They're all essential song ideas, situations, stories or concepts that give you pretty much free rein to turn that initial spark into a completed song. As I said, I'm not going to give you tons of explanation on what you could do with each idea, though sometimes I've thrown in an extra sentence or two where I thought it would help.

Most of these starters need a bit of fleshing out to become complete song ideas. That is, you'll want to figure out who specifically is singing, who they're singing to, and what they're trying to say. So it's worth giving that some thought before you do anything else.

From there, it's a good idea to decide on a lyrical hook or title – a word or phrase that neatly summarizes your song's message – and then build your lyric around that. Meanwhile, you'll want to think about grooves, chord progressions and a vocal melody that supports and helps to communicate the song's fundamental idea or message.

You can build all those parts of the song in whatever order you like, but the key – as in all of the starter types – is to put those pieces together in a way that works as an effective whole. And by starting with an idea or concept, you get the centerpiece or cornerstone that's going to tie all the different parts of your song together – the thing that it's about – so you can build the song out from there.

WORD STARTERS

Word starters are not a world away from idea starters, but they take things a bit further back to basics: they give you a single word or short phrase you can use to build a complete song.

They look like this:

pain

*Use this word or phrase in your song's title or part of its lyric,
then build a complete song around that.*

So the word 'pain' could inspire a song titled 'Feel My Pain' or 'Addicted to Pain' or 'The Pain Train' or even – if you can think of a strong concept to go with it – just 'Pain' itself. With all of these starters you can also use a closely related word, like 'pains' or 'pained' or 'painful', if that helps you incorporate the word in the song's title or an important phrase in its lyric.

There are tons of this type of starter in this book – nearly a third of all the starters here – because they're so simple but open up so many possibilities. And the words you get definitely aren't random: I chose them all because they're rich in nuance, depth or meaning, and all hint at compelling situations, concepts or stories you could build an interesting song around.

And just like with the idea starters, you'll want to think about your song's specific situation – who's singing, who they're singing to, what they're saying – while you figure out a specific phrase that incorporates the word or words of the song starter. That means you'll probably have to invent a handful of details to flesh out your song's situation or story, to give you a solid foundation to write from.

Once you've got that, like with the idea starters, you can then turn that idea or concept into a complete song. There are no rules about how or where you should use each word, but whatever you do it's worth thinking about using them somewhere important or prominent in the song. The song's title is one of the most obvious and effective places, but you can do something different if that feels right for the song you have in mind.

CHORD STARTERS

Chord starters are exactly what you'd expect – 4- or 8-measure chord progressions you can use somewhere in a song.

They look like this:

C – Am – F – G

C major: **I – vi – IV – V**

Write a song that uses this chord progression.

Using them might mean just repeating the chords over and over and calling that your song's chord progression. It might mean using them in your song's verse or chorus but writing your own chords for other sections. Or it might mean using the chords as part of a larger chord progression somewhere in your song.

For each of the progressions, you'll get the chords in a specific, voice-friendly key, but you'll also get the functional (Roman numeral) notation that describe each chord's function within that key. (There's an Appendix at the back of the book that explains what these symbols mean if you need any help with that.)

You can absolutely use each chord progression exactly as is, but if you can and want to, you're also welcome to transpose it or mix up the basic chords with things like sevenths and other chord extensions, suspended chords and/or inversions.

Whatever you do, the trick to getting started with these chord progressions is to figure out the kind of instrumental groove you want, and then figure out some kind of song situation that goes with them. (Actually, there's nothing to stop you combining, say, an idea starter with a chord progression starter to create an über-starter if you want to.)

As usual, you're trying to make sure everything works together as a unified whole – like an upbeat groove with an upbeat message, or a ballad groove with an emotional message, or whatever. None of the chord progressions comes with styles, moods or tempos, so you can play around with different choices until you end up with something that works for each particular song.

You might decide on a groove and then figure out a song idea, or figure out a song idea and then use the chord progression to build a groove that fits it – whatever you like. All that matters is that all those things fit well together in the end.

Some of the chord progressions come from well-known songs and some don't. Some are super simple and some are richer and more interesting. Most have one chord per measure, but a few mix that pattern up a bit, so it'll be up to you how to split the two chords across the bar where necessary.

If you're feeling extra adventurous, you could even tweak the harmonic rhythm – the rhythm of the chord changes – of some of the chord starters so they last a different number of measures or the chords are spread differently over the four or eight measures. (Though they work great, as is, of course.)

RHYTHM STARTERS

Rhythmic starters give you the skeleton of a musical idea – a rhythm of two or four measures you could use to build a groove, vocal melody, instrumental hook, anything, somewhere in your song.

They look like this:

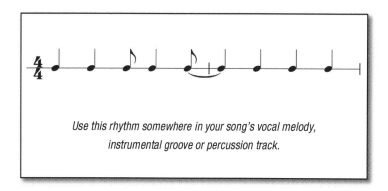

Use this rhythm somewhere in your song's vocal melody,
instrumental groove or percussion track.

They're basic enough they could form tons of different parts of a song. I toyed with giving you some specific melodic starters instead, but it was hard to come up with any that worked in a range of styles and feels – so with these rhythms you've got plenty of room to play around and see where they work best.

The rhythm starters are short enough that you'll have to extend, develop or repeat them somehow to make them into complete musical phrases or ideas. You might want to put the rhythm in one specific part or track or split it between a few. As you work through them, you'll also get a feel for which ones work best as vocal melodies, guitar grooves, bass riffs, drum tracks or whatever – because for all the freedom you have to use the rhythms anywhere, not every rhythm will work well everywhere.

To build fuller ideas out of each starter, a great way to begin is to start tapping, playing or singing each rhythm and trying to get inside the feel it's giving you. Then try and build complete rhythmic phrases – whether they end up becoming a bass part, vocal melody – instinctively out of what you've got. From there you can build even longer phrases or sections, thinking about how to repeat or develop each rhythm in a way that feels natural and intuitive to you. (That's really important with rhythm – you want to feel that it's right, that it fits.)

For example, you could turn one rhythm into a groove pattern and spin that out over a four-chord progression. Or you could turn it into a drum track and build the rest of your groove on top of that. You could then use those parts to form part or all of your song's verse, chorus, bridge or intro – whichever part seems to make the most sense.

Once you've done that, the same applies with every other starter – you're trying to put all the other parts of your song together in a way that makes sense as a unified whole. Depending how you use it, each rhythm will suggest a particular style or mood for your song, and it's up to you to find an overall song idea that fits that well.

Most of the rhythm starters are in 4/4, because the vast majority of songs are in 4/4, but there are plenty in other meters also – including a couple of exotic ones – to keep you on your toes. If you don't read notation or just want to be sure you've interpreted each rhythm correctly, you can also get hold of recordings of each of the rhythm starters at **thesongfoundry.com/rhythm-starters**.

MISCELLANEOUS STARTERS

Finally, the miscellaneous starters are some of the most interesting – and potentially most stimulating – ways you can write new songs. They're basically tons of different and sometimes unusual ways of getting started that don't fit neatly into the other four categories.

They look like this:

Set a drum loop playing. Improvise a melody over the top until you find something you like. Then build a song around that.

Use this starting point or process to build a complete song.

They usually involve either starting with a more distinctive or particular catalyst for a song – or finding your own – then building the rest of the song around that.

That means there are a few technical musical terms lying around in these starters. There's nothing too obscure or advanced, but depending on your level of experience and knowledge of music theory, you can of course look anything up if you need to. And like all the other kinds of starters, some of them might turn out to be great ideas and some not so much – but that's how writing songs works, and it's another great reason to try different things out just to see where they take you.

As for how you're going to build complete songs out of these starters, to be honest, figuring that out as you write is 90% of the fun with them. They'll have you thinking about songwriting in different ways or approaching songwriting from fresh angles, so don't be afraid about using everything you know about songwriting already to carve out your own path from each initial idea to a finished song.

Like with the rest of the starters, it's often a good idea to figure out your song's big idea first – who and what it's about. Or you might let each starter lead to a groove or a chord melody or part of a song's lyric then let the rest of the song flow from that.

Either way, these are really fun starters for stretching yourself as a songwriter in new ways – so any time you're up for an adventure, just pick one of them and see what happens.

[WRITE]

THE 501 SONG STARTERS

"A journey of a thousand miles begins with a single step."

LAO TZU

"The scariest moment is always just before you start."

STEPHEN KING

"Ah $&%! it, let's do it."

ANYONE WHO EVER ACHIEVED ANYTHING,

LIKE, EVER

[1]
IDEA STARTER

Write a song that says 'I love you.' Think about finding a specific and fresh way of expressing that idea, as well as a specific situation to explore it through.

Use this idea, situation or concept to build a complete song.

[2]
CHORD STARTER

C – F – G – F

C major: I – IV – V – IV

Write a song that uses this chord progression.

[3]
WORD STARTER

inside

Use this word or phrase in your song's title or part of its lyric, then build a complete song around that.

[4]
RHYTHM STARTER

Use this rhythm somewhere in your song's vocal melody, instrumental groove or percussion track.

[5]
IDEA STARTER

Write a song that says 'I don't love you anymore.' Think about what happened that changed your singer's attitude and make sure the song explains that.

Use this idea, situation or concept to build a complete song.

[6]
WORD STARTER

found

Use this word or phrase in your song's title or part of its lyric, then build a complete song around that.

[7]
MISCELLANEOUS STARTER

Write a song with a one-word title – like 'Hello', 'Tomorrow' or 'Fascination'.

Use this starting point or process to build a complete song.

[8]
WORD STARTER

tease

Use this word or phrase in your song's title or part of its lyric, then build a complete song around that.

[9]

CHORD STARTER

D – G – D – A

D major: I – IV – I – V

Write a song that uses this chord progression.

[10]

RHYTHM STARTER

Use this rhythm somewhere in your song's vocal melody,
instrumental groove or percussion track.

[11]
WORD STARTER

stone

Use this word or phrase in your song's title or part of its lyric, then build a complete song around that.

[12]
IDEA STARTER

Write a song that says 'I want to love you, but I can't.'
Come up with a specific and compelling situation where someone has conflicting or mixed feelings and make sure it's clear why.

Use this idea, situation or concept to build a complete song.

[13]
WORD STARTER

hollow

Use this word or phrase in your song's title or part of its lyric, then build a complete song around that.

[14]
MISCELLANEOUS STARTER

Write a song with an abstract title – like 'Simple Song', 'One-Note Samba' or 'Song for Jane'.

Use this starting point or process to build a complete song.

[15]

CHORD STARTER

C – Am – F – G

C major: I – vi – IV – V

Write a song that uses this chord progression.

[16]

WORD STARTER

my turn

Use this word or phrase in your song's title or part of its lyric, then
build a complete song around that.

[17]
IDEA STARTER

Write a song that says 'I've never met anyone like you before.'

Use this idea, situation or concept to build a complete song.

[18]
RHYTHM STARTER

Use this rhythm somewhere in your song's vocal melody, instrumental groove or percussion track.

[19]
IDEA STARTER

Write a song that says 'I'm happy' – and have fun letting your
singer explain why.

Use this idea, situation or concept to build a complete song.

[20]
CHORD STARTER

C – Am – F – F

C major: **I – vi – IV – IV**

Write a song that uses this chord progression.

[21]
MISCELLANEOUS STARTER

Write a song with an unusual or original word or phrase as its title – like 'Versace on the Floor', 'Wonderwall' or 'Strawberry Fields Forever'.

Use this starting point or process to build a complete song.

[22]
WORD STARTER

addiction

Use this word or phrase in your song's title or part of its lyric, then build a complete song around that.

[23]
IDEA STARTER

Write a song that says 'Show me some respect.'

Use this idea, situation or concept to build a complete song.

[24]
RHYTHM STARTER

*Use this rhythm somewhere in your song's vocal melody,
instrumental groove or percussion track.*

[25]
WORD STARTER

dumb

Use this word or phrase in your song's title or part of its lyric, then build a complete song around that.

[26]
IDEA STARTER

Write a song that says 'I'm not happy' – and make sure your singer explains why.

Use this idea, situation or concept to build a complete song.

[27]

CHORD STARTER

E – E – A – B

E major: I – I – IV – V

Write a song that uses this chord progression.

[28]

WORD STARTER

Ireland

Use this word or phrase in your song's title or part of its lyric, then build a complete song around that.

[29]
MISCELLANEOUS STARTER

Write a song that has a metaphor at its center – like ''Cos baby, you're a firework' or 'I am titanium.'

Use this starting point or process to build a complete song.

[30]
IDEA STARTER

Write a song that says 'I don't care' or 'I don't want to know.'

Use this idea, situation or concept to build a complete song.

[31]
WORD STARTER

problematic

Use this word or phrase in your song's title or part of its lyric, then build a complete song around that.

[32]
RHYTHM STARTER

Use this rhythm somewhere in your song's vocal melody, instrumental groove or percussion track.

[33]
IDEA STARTER

Write a song that says 'I don't know.' Pick a specific situation where not knowing something is significant, and make sure your audience understands why.

Use this idea, situation or concept to build a complete song.

[34]
WORD STARTER

oxygen

Use this word or phrase in your song's title or part of its lyric, then build a complete song around that.

[35]
CHORD STARTER

C – G – Am – F

C major: **I** – **V** – **vi** – **IV**

Write a song that uses this chord progression.

[36]
MISCELLANEOUS STARTER

Write a song that has a simile at its center – like 'You shine like a diamond' or 'Sweet like chocolate'.

Use this starting point or process to build a complete song.

[37]
WORD STARTER

macho

Use this word or phrase in your song's title or part of its lyric, then build a complete song around that.

[38]
IDEA STARTER

Write a song that asks 'Baby, what's wrong?'

Use this idea, situation or concept to build a complete song.

[39]
CHORD STARTER

Am – C – Dm – E

A minor: **i – III – iv – V**

Write a song that uses this chord progression.

[40]
WORD STARTER

elegance

*Use this word or phrase in your song's title or part of its lyric, then
build a complete song around that.*

[41]
IDEA STARTER

Write a song that says 'You let me down' or 'You betrayed me.'

Use this idea, situation or concept to build a complete song.

[42]
RHYTHM STARTER

Use this rhythm somewhere in your song's vocal melody,
instrumental groove or percussion track.

[43]
WORD STARTER

soul

Use this word or phrase in your song's title or part of its lyric, then build a complete song around that.

[44]
IDEA STARTER

Write a song that says 'Nothing's gonna stop me.'

Use this idea, situation or concept to build a complete song.

[45]
MISCELLANEOUS STARTER

Write a song that has a non-English word in its title. Pick any word you like, but for impact you probably want a word that would be understood by most English speakers. You could also use some related non-English words in other parts of the song.

Use this starting point or process to build a complete song.

[46]
CHORD STARTER

Em – C – Am – B

E minor: **i – VI – iv – V**

Write a song that uses this chord progression.

[47]
WORD STARTER

U-turn

Use this word or phrase in your song's title or part of its lyric, then build a complete song around that.

[48]
RHYTHM STARTER

Use this rhythm somewhere in your song's vocal melody, instrumental groove or percussion track.

[49]

MISCELLANEOUS STARTER

Write a song that uses the words 'ooh', 'oh' or 'ah' in a significant way. Do this any way you like, but incorporating them as a key part of your chorus lyric can be really effective.

Use this starting point or process to build a complete song.

[50]

WORD STARTER

pain

Use this word or phrase in your song's title or part of its lyric, then build a complete song around that.

[51]
CHORD STARTER

C – Am – F – G – Dm – E7 – Am – F

C major: I – vi – IV – V – ii – III7 – vi – IV

Write a song that uses this chord progression.

[52]
WORD STARTER

defenseless

Use this word or phrase in your song's title or part of its lyric, then build a complete song around that.

[53]
IDEA STARTER

Write a song that says 'No more holding myself back.'

Use this idea, situation or concept to build a complete song.

[54]
RHYTHM STARTER

Use this rhythm somewhere in your song's vocal melody,
instrumental groove or percussion track.

[55]
WORD STARTER

web

Use this word or phrase in your song's title or part of its lyric, then build a complete song around that.

[56]
IDEA STARTER

Write a song that lays down your ground rules for a successful relationship.

Use this idea, situation or concept to build a complete song.

[57]

MISCELLANEOUS STARTER

Write a song whose chorus features a single word or phrase repeated over and over. There are plenty of these songs around – Ariana Grande's 'thank u, next' is a good example – and this technique can be a great way of writing a catchy chorus.

Use this starting point or process to build a complete song.

[58]

WORD STARTER

set up

Use this word or phrase in your song's title or part of its lyric, then build a complete song around that.

[59]
CHORD STARTER

Am – B – E7 – Am

A minor: **i – II – V7 – i**

Write a song that uses this chord progression.

[60]
IDEA STARTER

Write a song that says 'I need your help.'

Use this idea, situation or concept to build a complete song.

[61]
WORD STARTER

official

Use this word or phrase in your song's title or part of its lyric, then build a complete song around that.

[62]
MISCELLANEOUS STARTER

Write a song that's no longer than 90 seconds. Use whatever structure you like and see this limitation as a challenge to make every word and note you write really count.

Use this starting point or process to build a complete song.

[63]
WORD STARTER

real life

Use this word or phrase in your song's title or part of its lyric, then build a complete song around that.

[64]
RHYTHM STARTER

Use this rhythm somewhere in your song's vocal melody, instrumental groove or percussion track.

[65]
IDEA STARTER

Write a song that lists the things you love about someone.
This could be a love song where the chorus is the list, or the chorus has a separate unifying message and the list becomes the raw material for the verses.

Use this idea, situation or concept to build a complete song.

[66]
CHORD STARTER

F – Dm – E♭ – B♭

F major: **I – vi – ♭VII – IV**

Write a song that uses this chord progression.

[67]
WORD STARTER

reason

Use this word or phrase in your song's title or part of its lyric, then build a complete song around that.

[68]
IDEA STARTER

Write a song that says 'I told you so.' Think about who's going to receive that message and what specifically your song's singer had warned them about.

Use this idea, situation or concept to build a complete song.

[69]

CHORD STARTER

G – C – Am – D

G major: **I – IV – ii – V**

Write a song that uses this chord progression.

[70]

WORD STARTER

freedom

Use this word or phrase in your song's title or part of its lyric, then build a complete song around that.

[71]
IDEA STARTER

Write a song that says 'You're the best thing that's ever happened to me.'

Use this idea, situation or concept to build a complete song.

[72]
WORD STARTER

life and death

Use this word or phrase in your song's title or part of its lyric, then build a complete song around that.

[73]
CHORD STARTER

C – C/E – F – F – C – C/E – Dm F – G

C major: **I – Ib – IV – IV – I – Ib – ii IV – V**

Write a song that uses this chord progression.

[74]
RHYTHM STARTER

*Use this rhythm somewhere in your song's vocal melody,
instrumental groove or percussion track.*

[75]
IDEA STARTER

Write a song that says 'I deserve better.'

Use this idea, situation or concept to build a complete song.

[76]
WORD STARTER

merry-go-round

Use this word or phrase in your song's title or part of its lyric, then build a complete song around that.

[77]
MISCELLANEOUS STARTER

Write a song that uses hardly any rhymes, or even no rhymes at all. To compensate for the lack of rhyme, think about using a repetitive line and syllable structure, and techniques like assonance and consonance to bind your song lyric together more subtly.

Use this starting point or process to build a complete song.

[78]
WORD STARTER

deep

Use this word or phrase in your song's title or part of its lyric, then build a complete song around that.

[79]
CHORD STARTER

Am G/B – C – F C – G

C major: **vi Vb – I – IV I – V**

Write a song that uses this chord progression.

[80]
RHYTHM STARTER

*Use this rhythm somewhere in your song's vocal melody,
instrumental groove or percussion track.*

[81]

WORD STARTER

sensation

Use this word or phrase in your song's title or part of its lyric, then build a complete song around that.

[82]

IDEA STARTER

Write a song that says 'I need a fresh start.' Think about what your singer wants a fresh start from, as well as what happened or is happening that made them decide that.

Use this idea, situation or concept to build a complete song.

[83]
WORD STARTER

reaction

Use this word or phrase in your song's title or part of its lyric, then build a complete song around that.

[84]
MISCELLANEOUS STARTER

Set a drum loop playing. Improvise a melody over the top until you find something you like. Then build a song around that.

Use this starting point or process to build a complete song.

[85]
WORD STARTER

Write a love duet for two people who feel exactly the same way.

Use this idea, situation or concept to build a complete song.

[86]
CHORD STARTER

Am – F – C – G

A minor: **i – VI – III – VII**

Write a song that uses this chord progression.

[87]
WORD STARTER

black

Use this word or phrase in your song's title or part of its lyric, then build a complete song around that.

[88]
RHYTHM STARTER

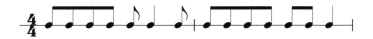

Use this rhythm somewhere in your song's vocal melody, instrumental groove or percussion track.

[89]
IDEA STARTER

Write a love duet for two people who feel slightly differently. Try to center the song around a subtle but specific difference your two singers have in their attitudes and/or perspectives.

Use this idea, situation or concept to build a complete song.

[90]
WORD STARTER

dragon

Use this word or phrase in your song's title or part of its lyric, then build a complete song around that.

[91]
IDEA STARTER

Write a love duet for two people who feel significantly different about their relationship. Think about the contrasting attitudes or perspectives your singers could have, and try to use them to make your song's situation really compelling.

Use this idea, situation or concept to build a complete song.

[92]
WORD STARTER

show

Use this word or phrase in your song's title or part of its lyric, then build a complete song around that.

[93]

CHORD STARTER

Am – G – F – G

A minor: **i – VII – VI – VII**

Write a song that uses this chord progression.

[94]

MISCELLANEOUS STARTER

Write a song with a lyric that never uses the letter 'p'. That might sound like a crazy challenge, but the restriction can help you write something interesting you wouldn't have written otherwise.

Use this starting point or process to build a complete song.

[95]
WORD STARTER

neon

*Use this word or phrase in your song's title or part of its lyric, then
build a complete song around that.*

[96]
RHYTHM STARTER

*Use this rhythm somewhere in your song's vocal melody,
instrumental groove or percussion track.*

[97]
IDEA STARTER

Write a love duet where two partners start with different opinions but end up closer by the end. Think about how that change progresses throughout your song's structure. Pick any reversal you like, but subtle ones are usually easier to pull off.

Use this idea, situation or concept to build a complete song.

[98]
WORD STARTER

restless

Use this word or phrase in your song's title or part of its lyric, then build a complete song around that.

[99]
IDEA STARTER

Write a breakup song where the singer is sad to break up.

Use this idea, situation or concept to build a complete song.

[100]
WORD STARTER

word

*Use this word or phrase in your song's title or part of its lyric, then
build a complete song around that.*

[101]
MISCELLANEOUS STARTER

Write a song where no lyric line has more than five words.
Simplicity is an essential tool in songwriting, and writing with this
constraint will help you laser-focus your song's message.

Use this starting point or process to build a complete song.

[102]
CHORD STARTER

C – Dm – F – G

C major: I – ii – IV – V

Write a song that uses this chord progression.

[103]
WORD STARTER

nothing

Use this word or phrase in your song's title or part of its lyric, then build a complete song around that.

[104]
RHYTHM STARTER

Use this rhythm somewhere in your song's vocal melody, instrumental groove or percussion track.

[105]
CHORD STARTER

Dm – B♭ – C – Dm

D minor: **i – VI – VII – i**

Write a song that uses this chord progression.

[106]
IDEA STARTER

Write a breakup song where the singer is glad to be breaking up.

Use this idea, situation or concept to build a complete song.

[107]
WORD STARTER

zip

*Use this word or phrase in your song's title or part of its lyric, then
build a complete song around that.*

[108]
RHYTHM STARTER

*Use this rhythm somewhere in your song's vocal melody,
instrumental groove or percussion track.*

[109]
CHORD STARTER

C – Bm7♭5 E7 – Am – F G

C major: I – vii7♭5 III7 – vi – IV V

Write a song that uses this chord progression.

[110]
WORD STARTER

finesse

Use this word or phrase in your song's title or part of its lyric, then build a complete song around that.

[111]
IDEA STARTER

Write a breakup song where the singer is conflicted about breaking up. Try to come up with a specific situation where things are complicated for your singer, or where they just have doubts about their decision.

Use this idea, situation or concept to build a complete song.

[112]
WORD STARTER

liar

Use this word or phrase in your song's title or part of its lyric, then build a complete song around that.

[113]
MISCELLANEOUS STARTER

Stick your index fingers at two random points in a novel or short story. Incorporate the two words you pointed to into some kind of interesting phrase, then write a song that uses that phrase as its title.

Use this starting point or process to build a complete song.

[114]
IDEA STARTER

Write a post-breakup song that says 'I want you back.'

Use this idea, situation or concept to build a complete song.

[115]
WORD STARTER

echo

Use this word or phrase in your song's title or part of its lyric, then build a complete song around that.

[116]
IDEA STARTER

Write a post-breakup song that says 'I definitely don't want you back.' Think about the specific situation or chain of events that led your singer to decide that.

Use this idea, situation or concept to build a complete song.

[117]
CHORD STARTER

C – D/C C – Bm7 – Em

G major: **IV – V/4 IV – iii7 – vi**

Write a song that uses this chord progression.

[118]
WORD STARTER

physical

Use this word or phrase in your song's title or part of its lyric, then build a complete song around that.

[119]
IDEA STARTER

Write a third-person song that tells the story of someone you think is really interesting. Make sure the song focuses on what you find interesting about them.

Use this idea, situation or concept to build a complete song.

[120]
RHYTHM STARTER

Use this rhythm somewhere in your song's vocal melody, instrumental groove or percussion track.

[121]
WORD STARTER

intimate

*Use this word or phrase in your song's title or part of its lyric, then
build a complete song around that.*

[122]
MISCELLANEOUS STARTER

**Write a song that uses an acronym as its title. You could invent
an interesting new one – like 'P.Y.T. (Pretty Young Thing)' did –
or choose an existing acronym, like TLC, LTR or MCM.**

Use this starting point or process to build a complete song.

[123]
IDEA STARTER

Write a third-person song that tells the story of someone you think is misunderstood. See if you can change our minds about that person.

Use this idea, situation or concept to build a complete song.

[124]
WORD STARTER

boomerang

Use this word or phrase in your song's title or part of its lyric, then build a complete song around that.

[125]

CHORD STARTER

C – C E7 – Am – F Fm

C major: I – I III7 – vi – IV iv

Write a song that uses this chord progression.

[126]

IDEA STARTER

Write a third-person song that tells the story of someone you dislike. Try to cast the song in a way that's engaging, unique or humorous enough that it doesn't just feel like a rant.

Use this idea, situation or concept to build a complete song.

[127]
MISCELLANEOUS STARTER

Find a real-life story in a newspaper or on a news site that captivates or interests you. Write a song about or inspired by it.

Use this starting point or process to build a complete song.

[128]
WORD STARTER

sisterhood

Use this word or phrase in your song's title or part of its lyric, then build a complete song around that.

[129]
RHYTHM STARTER

*Use this rhythm somewhere in your song's vocal melody,
instrumental groove or percussion track.*

[130]
IDEA STARTER

**Write a third-person song that tells the story of someone
you know personally.** Choose a specific situation that includes
them and explain what's interesting or different about it.

Use this idea, situation or concept to build a complete song.

[131]
WORD STARTER

meanwhile

Use this word or phrase in your song's title or part of its lyric, then build a complete song around that.

[132]
CHORD STARTER

C – C/E – F – Fm

C major: **I – Ib – IV – iv**

Write a song that uses this chord progression.

[133]
WORD STARTER

ace

Use this word or phrase in your song's title or part of its lyric, then build a complete song around that.

[134]
RHYTHM STARTER

Use this rhythm somewhere in your song's vocal melody, instrumental groove or percussion track.

[135]
MISCELLANEOUS STARTER

Look through the fiction section of a physical or online bookstore. Find a book title you like the sound of, then write a song with the same title.

Use this starting point or process to build a complete song.

[136]
CHORD STARTER

B♭ – C – Am – Dm

F major: **IV – V – iii – vi**

Write a song that uses this chord progression.

[137]
IDEA STARTER

Write a third-person song that tells the story of a well-known historical or living person. Try to focus on what's remarkable about them or their story.

Use this idea, situation or concept to build a complete song.

[138]
WORD STARTER

bingo

Use this word or phrase in your song's title or part of its lyric, then build a complete song around that.

[139]
IDEA STARTER

Write a song that warns someone about someone else.
Think about the specific situation: who is involved, what the
singer is warning the other person about, and how they found it
out.

Use this idea, situation or concept to build a complete song.

[140]
WORD STARTER

rainy

*Use this word or phrase in your song's title or part of its lyric, then
build a complete song around that.*

[141]

CHORD STARTER

C – Em – F – Gsus4 G

C major: **I – iii – IV – Vsus4 V**

Write a song that uses this chord progression.

[142]

IDEA STARTER

Write a song about a rumor. It could be a rumor your singer heard first-hand or one someone else told your singer that directly affected them.

Use this idea, situation or concept to build a complete song.

[143]
WORD STARTER

mean

Use this word or phrase in your song's title or part of its lyric, then build a complete song around that.

[144]
RHYTHM STARTER

Use this rhythm somewhere in your song's vocal melody, instrumental groove or percussion track.

[145]
MISCELLANEOUS STARTER

Tear out a page from a magazine or newspaper. Cut out up to ten words that sound interesting to you from the page. Play around with those words on a flat surface, reordering them until they suggest a title and/or part of a chorus lyric to you.

Use this starting point or process to build a complete song.

[146]
WORD STARTER

interrupted

Use this word or phrase in your song's title or part of its lyric, then build a complete song around that.

[147]
CHORD STARTER

D – E7 – A – D D/C♯ – Bm – Em – A7 – D

D major: I – II7 – V – I I/7 – vi – ii – V7 – I

Write a song that uses this chord progression.

[148]
WORD STARTER

astray

Use this word or phrase in your song's title or part of its lyric, then build a complete song around that.

[149]
IDEA STARTER

Write a song that introduces you (or someone else) as an artist to the world.

Use this idea, situation or concept to build a complete song.

[150]
RHYTHM STARTER

*Use this rhythm somewhere in your song's vocal melody,
instrumental groove or percussion track.*

[151]
WORD STARTER

island

Use this word or phrase in your song's title or part of its lyric, then build a complete song around that.

[152]
MISCELLANEOUS STARTER

Next time you're out in public, listen out for interesting stories or conflicts from the people around you. When you overhear something interesting, write a song based on it.

Use this starting point or process to build a complete song.

[153]
IDEA STARTER

Write a song where the singer makes clear one or more reasons they're different or unique – a song that says 'I'm worth paying attention to and here's why.'

Use this idea, situation or concept to build a complete song.

[154]
WORD STARTER

doubt

Use this word or phrase in your song's title or part of its lyric, then build a complete song around that.

[155]
IDEA STARTER

Write a song where the singer sets the record straight or addresses a common misconception about them – a song that says 'What you probably think isn't true and here's why.'

Use this idea, situation or concept to build a complete song.

[156]
CHORD STARTER

G – Am/G – G – D

G major: **I – ii/1 – I – V**

Write a song that uses this chord progression.

[157]
WORD STARTER

persistence

*Use this word or phrase in your song's title or part of its lyric, then
build a complete song around that.*

[158]
RHYTHM STARTER

*Use this rhythm somewhere in your song's vocal melody,
instrumental groove or percussion track.*

[159]
IDEA STARTER

Write a song about one of your key life philosophies —
something you believe that keeps proving itself important or
helpful to you.

Use this idea, situation or concept to build a complete song.

[160]
WORD STARTER

irregular

*Use this word or phrase in your song's title or part of its lyric, then
build a complete song around that.*

[161]
MISCELLANEOUS STARTER

Write a song that responds to an existing song from the recipient's perspective – think about who the original song is sung to and write a new song that lets that person respond.

Use this starting point or process to build a complete song.

[162]
CHORD STARTER

F – Dm C/E – F – Csus4 C

F major: **I – vi Vb – I – Vsus4 V**

Write a song that uses this chord progression.

[163]
WORD STARTER

lost

Use this word or phrase in your song's title or part of its lyric, then build a complete song around that.

[164]
CHORD STARTER

F – Em – Am – G

C major: **IV – iii – vi – V**

Write a song that uses this chord progression.

[165]
MISCELLANEOUS STARTER

Take the title of an existing song, but write a completely different song using that title. The key here is finding a completely different song situation or story that is still supported by that title.

Use this starting point or process to build a complete song.

[166]
WORD STARTER

property

Use this word or phrase in your song's title or part of its lyric, then build a complete song around that.

[167]
IDEA STARTER

Write a song about a major change or event in your life.

Use this idea, situation or concept to build a complete song.

[168]
WORD STARTER

surprise

*Use this word or phrase in your song's title or part of its lyric, then
build a complete song around that.*

[169]
RHYTHM STARTER

*Use this rhythm somewhere in your song's vocal melody,
instrumental groove or percussion track.*

[170]
MISCELLANEOUS STARTER

**Pick a song that you think misses the point or doesn't ring true.
Write your own song that addresses that.** For example, you might
disagree with the idea that 'All you need is love'.

Use this starting point or process to build a complete song.

[171]
WORD STARTER

dollar

Use this word or phrase in your song's title or part of its lyric, then build a complete song around that.

[172]
CHORD STARTER

Bm – F♯ – G – D D/C♯

B minor: **i – V – VI – III III/2**

Write a song that uses this chord progression.

[173]
IDEA STARTER

Write a song about your biggest hope in life.

Use this idea, situation or concept to build a complete song.

[174]
WORD STARTER

spot on

Use this word or phrase in your song's title or part of its lyric, then build a complete song around that.

[175]
IDEA STARTER

Write a song about your biggest fear in life.

Use this idea, situation or concept to build a complete song.

[176]
CHORD STARTER

C – G/B – Am – D

G major: **IV – Ib – ii – V**

Write a song that uses this chord progression.

[177]
WORD STARTER

grasp

Use this word or phrase in your song's title or part of its lyric, then build a complete song around that.

[178]
RHYTHM STARTER

Use this rhythm somewhere in your song's vocal melody, instrumental groove or percussion track.

[179]
IDEA STARTER

Write a song about growing up in your neighborhood – try
and focus it around a specific idea, message or story.

Use this idea, situation or concept to build a complete song.

[180]
WORD STARTER

belong

*Use this word or phrase in your song's title or part of its lyric, then
build a complete song around that.*

[181]
MISCELLANEOUS STARTER

Pick an existing song that has a title of at least three words. Change one of those words then write your own song with that title.

Use this starting point or process to build a complete song.

[182]
RHYTHM STARTER

Use this rhythm somewhere in your song's vocal melody, instrumental groove or percussion track.

[183]
WORD STARTER

style

Use this word or phrase in your song's title or part of its lyric, then build a complete song around that.

[184]
CHORD STARTER

C – Dm/C – C – G/B – Am – F – C – Gsus4

C major: **I – ii/1 – I – Vb – vi – IV – I – Vsus4**

Write a song that uses this chord progression.

[185]
IDEA STARTER

Write a song about a major event in your life, but from someone else's perspective. Think about not just what that event is, but why the perspective you choose makes the song interesting.

Use this idea, situation or concept to build a complete song.

[186]
WORD STARTER

within

Use this word or phrase in your song's title or part of its lyric, then build a complete song around that.

[187]
IDEA STARTER

Write a song that makes people happy – think about a specific situation or a fresh message that inspires people or lifts them up.

Use this idea, situation or concept to build a complete song.

[188]
WORD STARTER

knuckle

Use this word or phrase in your song's title or part of its lyric, then build a complete song around that.

[189]
CHORD STARTER

F – C/E – Dm – C

C major: **IV – Ib – ii – I**

Write a song that uses this chord progression.

[190]
MISCELLANEOUS STARTER

Write a song in a genre or style you've never tried writing in before. Do some research – listen around in the genre if you need some inspiration to get started.

Use this starting point or process to build a complete song.

[191]
WORD STARTER

illuminate

Use this word or phrase in your song's title or part of its lyric, then build a complete song around that.

[192]
IDEA STARTER

Write a song that makes people feel compassion for someone who's suffering.

Use this idea, situation or concept to build a complete song.

[193]
RHYTHM STARTER

*Use this rhythm somewhere in your song's vocal melody,
instrumental groove or percussion track.*

[194]
WORD STARTER

south

*Use this word or phrase in your song's title or part of its lyric, then
build a complete song around that.*

[195]
IDEA STARTER

Write a song that makes people laugh. It could be a song about a funny person or a funny thing that happened, or just a song with an amusing message or twist.

Use this idea, situation or concept to build a complete song.

[196]
WORD STARTER

Chinese whispers

Use this word or phrase in your song's title or part of its lyric, then build a complete song around that.

[197]
IDEA STARTER

Write a song that makes people want to dance. You've got plenty of opportunity in both your song's groove and lyric to encourage people to bust some moves.

Use this idea, situation or concept to build a complete song.

[198]
RHYTHM STARTER

Use this rhythm somewhere in your song's vocal melody, instrumental groove or percussion track.

[199]
WORD STARTER

honor

Use this word or phrase in your song's title or part of its lyric, then build a complete song around that.

[200]
CHORD STARTER

Dm – Em – F – G

C major: **ii – iii – IV – V**

Write a song that uses this chord progression.

[201]
IDEA STARTER

Write a song about partying on a weekend.

Use this idea, situation or concept to build a complete song.

[202]
MISCELLANEOUS STARTER

Write a song that fuses two genres or styles that don't often go together. Think about which genres or styles could work and also which specific elements of each you want to to combine.

Use this starting point or process to build a complete song.

[203]
WORD STARTER

unwritten

Use this word or phrase in your song's title or part of its lyric, then build a complete song around that.

[204]
IDEA STARTER

Write a song that encourages people to say 'I love you' more.

Use this idea, situation or concept to build a complete song.

[205]
MISCELLANEOUS STARTER

Write a chorus vocal melody that's especially simple, then build a complete song around that.

Use this starting point or process to build a complete song.

[206]
WORD STARTER

forgive

Use this word or phrase in your song's title or part of its lyric, then build a complete song around that.

[207]
CHORD STARTER

Am – Dm – G – C – F – Bm7♭5 –

Esus4 – E

A minor: **i – iv – VII – III – VI – ii7♭5 – Vsus4 – V**

Write a song that uses this chord progression.

[208]
RHYTHM STARTER

*Use this rhythm somewhere in your song's vocal melody,
instrumental groove or percussion track.*

[209]
IDEA STARTER

Write a song that motivates people to go after their goals.
Think about the specific message you want to share, plus any
specific examples or ideas you're going to include to explore
that message.

Use this idea, situation or concept to build a complete song.

[210]
WORD STARTER

beneath

*Use this word or phrase in your song's title or part of its lyric, then
build a complete song around that.*

[211]
IDEA STARTER

Write a song that tells people they don't have to put up with something they don't like.

Use this idea, situation or concept to build a complete song.

[212]
WORD STARTER

original

Use this word or phrase in your song's title or part of its lyric, then build a complete song around that.

[213]
MISCELLANEOUS STARTER

Write a chorus vocal melody that's as repetitive as you can make it without it being boring, then build a complete song around that.

Use this starting point or process to build a complete song.

[214]
CHORD STARTER

C – Am – B♭ – G

C major: I – vi – ♭VII – V

Write a song that uses this chord progression.

[215]
WORD STARTER

inhibition

Use this word or phrase in your song's title or part of its lyric, then build a complete song around that.

[216]
RHYTHM STARTER

Use this rhythm somewhere in your song's vocal melody, instrumental groove or percussion track.

[217]
IDEA STARTER

Write a song that encourages people to be themselves.

Use this idea, situation or concept to build a complete song.

[218]
CHORD STARTER

F – G/F – Em – Am

C major: **IV – Vd – iii – vi**

Write a song that uses this chord progression.

[219]
MISCELLANEOUS STARTER

Write a super catchy and repetitive riff – an instrumental figure of at least two measures that could be on guitar, bass or keys. Then build a complete song around that.

Use this starting point or process to build a complete song.

[220]
WORD STARTER

lead

(either the action or the metal)

Use this word or phrase in your song's title or part of its lyric, then build a complete song around that.

[221]
IDEA STARTER

Write a Public Service Announcement song of your choice –
a song with some kind of message that everyone should know
or think about.

Use this idea, situation or concept to build a complete song.

[222]
RHYTHM STARTER

Use this rhythm somewhere in your song's vocal melody,
instrumental groove or percussion track.

[223]
WORD STARTER

religion

Use this word or phrase in your song's title or part of its lyric, then build a complete song around that.

[224]
IDEA STARTER

Write a song that says 'You messed up big time.'

Use this idea, situation or concept to build a complete song.

[225]
WORD STARTER

fire

Use this word or phrase in your song's title or part of its lyric, then build a complete song around that.

[226]
CHORD STARTER

C – G/C – F/C G/C – C

C major: I – V/1 – IV/1 V/1 – I

Write a song that uses this chord progression.

[227]
IDEA STARTER

Write a song that says 'You messed up big time, but I forgive you.'

Use this idea, situation or concept to build a complete song.

[228]
RHYTHM STARTER

Use this rhythm somewhere in your song's vocal melody,
instrumental groove or percussion track.

[229]
WORD STARTER

boom

*Use this word or phrase in your song's title or part of its lyric, then
build a complete song around that.*

[230]
IDEA STARTER

**Write a song that says 'I messed up big time, and I'm
sorry.'** Tell us about exactly what happened and why your
singer feels the need to apologize.

Use this idea, situation or concept to build a complete song.

[231]

CHORD STARTER

C – F – Em – Dm

C major: I – IV – iii – ii

Write a song that uses this chord progression.

[232]

WORD STARTER

rock bottom

Use this word or phrase in your song's title or part of its lyric, then build a complete song around that.

[233]

IDEA STARTER

Write a song that says 'I'm not sorry.' Make it clear what happened and why your singer won't apologize for it.

Use this idea, situation or concept to build a complete song.

[234]

MISCELLANEOUS STARTER

Write a song with an upbeat tempo – anything you like, as long as its tempo is pretty quick.

Use this starting point or process to build a complete song.

[235]
IDEA STARTER

Write a song that says 'You're just jealous.'

Use this idea, situation or concept to build a complete song.

[236]
WORD STARTER

villain

Use this word or phrase in your song's title or part of its lyric, then build a complete song around that.

[237]
CHORD STARTER

C – F♯m7♭5 – F – G

C major: I – ♯iv7♭5 – IV – V

Write a song that uses this chord progression.

[238]
IDEA STARTER

Write a song that says 'Damn, I'm jealous.'

Use this idea, situation or concept to build a complete song.

[239]
MISCELLANEOUS STARTER

Write a ballad song – anything you like, as long as its tempo is
pretty slow.

Use this starting point or process to build a complete song.

[240]
RHYTHM STARTER

*Use this rhythm somewhere in your song's vocal melody,
instrumental groove or percussion track.*

[241]
IDEA STARTER

Write a song that says 'Leave me alone.'

Use this idea, situation or concept to build a complete song.

[242]
WORD STARTER

mortal

Use this word or phrase in your song's title or part of its lyric, then build a complete song around that.

[243]
CHORD STARTER

Am – F – G – Em

A minor: **i – VI – VII – v**

Write a song that uses this chord progression.

[244]
IDEA STARTER

Write a song that says 'Don't leave me alone.'

Use this idea, situation or concept to build a complete song.

[245]
WORD STARTER

forever

Use this word or phrase in your song's title or part of its lyric, then build a complete song around that.

[246]
MISCELLANEOUS STARTER

Write a funky groove, then build a complete song around that.

Use this starting point or process to build a complete song.

[247]
IDEA STARTER

Write a song that says 'I never want to see you again.'
That's a pretty dramatic statement, so make sure you explain
exactly why your singer feels that way.

Use this idea, situation or concept to build a complete song.

[248]
RHYTHM STARTER

*Use this rhythm somewhere in your song's vocal melody,
instrumental groove or percussion track.*

[249]
CHORD STARTER

Gm – Cm – B♭ – E♭ – D – D7/F♯ – Gm –

E♭ D

G minor: **i – iv – III – VI – V – V7b – I – VI V**

Write a song that uses this chord progression.

[250]
WORD STARTER

hopeless

Use this word or phrase in your song's title or part of its lyric, then build a complete song around that.

[251]
IDEA STARTER

Write a song that asks 'Is this what you wanted?'

Use this idea, situation or concept to build a complete song.

[252]
RHYTHM STARTER

Use this rhythm somewhere in your song's vocal melody,
instrumental groove or percussion track.

[253]
IDEA STARTER

Write a song that says 'Grow up.'

Use this idea, situation or concept to build a complete song.

[254]
WORD STARTER

perspective

Use this word or phrase in your song's title or part of its lyric, then build a complete song around that.

[255]
CHORD STARTER

Dm – Gm – C#dim – Dm

D minor: **i – iv – #vii° – i**

Write a song that uses this chord progression.

[256]
WORD STARTER

pure

Use this word or phrase in your song's title or part of its lyric, then build a complete song around that.

[257]
MISCELLANEOUS STARTER

Write a quirky or fun groove, then build a complete song around that.

Use this starting point or process to build a complete song.

[258]
IDEA STARTER

Write a song that asks 'Why?' It could be directed to a particular person, or it could be an abstract question to the universe. Whatever you pick, make it clear why the singer wants to know.

Use this idea, situation or concept to build a complete song.

[259]
WORD STARTER

imperfect

Use this word or phrase in your song's title or part of its lyric, then build a complete song around that.

[260]
CHORD STARTER

F – F G – Am – Am Em

C major: **IV – IV V – vi – vi iii**

Write a song that uses this chord progression.

[261]
IDEA STARTER

Write a song that says 'I'm afraid.' Think about what specifically the singer is afraid of, and give us some idea why.

Use this idea, situation or concept to build a complete song.

[262]
WORD STARTER

favorite

Use this word or phrase in your song's title or part of its lyric, then build a complete song around that.

[263]
MISCELLANEOUS STARTER

Write an intense or insistent groove, then build a complete song around that.

Use this starting point or process to build a complete song.

[264]
RHYTHM STARTER

*Use this rhythm somewhere in your song's vocal melody,
instrumental groove or percussion track.*

[265]
WORD STARTER

moral

Use this word or phrase in your song's title or part of its lyric, then build a complete song around that.

[266]
CHORD STARTER

C – E♭ – F – G

C major: I – ♭III – IV – V

Write a song that uses this chord progression.

[267]
IDEA STARTER

Write a song that tells someone to stop or slow down.

Use this idea, situation or concept to build a complete song.

[268]
WORD STARTER

impractical

Use this word or phrase in your song's title or part of its lyric, then build a complete song around that.

[269]

CHORD STARTER

E – B – A – A

E major: I – V – IV – IV

Write a song that uses this chord progression.

[270]

WORD STARTER

make a move

Use this word or phrase in your song's title or part of its lyric, then build a complete song around that.

[271]
CHORD STARTER

Am – Dm – F – E

A minor: **i – iv – VI – V**

Write a song that uses this chord progression.

[272]
IDEA STARTER

Write a song that says 'I have issues.' They could be specific issues, or the singer could be speaking in general. The singer could be accepting or apologetic, or some combination of the two.

Use this idea, situation or concept to build a complete song.

[273]
RHYTHM STARTER

Use this rhythm somewhere in your song's vocal melody,
instrumental groove or percussion track.

[274]
WORD STARTER

crush

Use this word or phrase in your song's title or part of its lyric, then
build a complete song around that.

[275]
IDEA STARTER

Write a song to someone who's afraid of a romantic commitment. Think about the specific message your singer is going to express. Will the song reassure the other person? Will it pressure them to commit? Or say the relationship can't work?

Use this idea, situation or concept to build a complete song.

[276]
RHYTHM STARTER

Use this rhythm somewhere in your song's vocal melody, instrumental groove or percussion track.

[277]
WORD STARTER

knockout

Use this word or phrase in your song's title or part of its lyric, then build a complete song around that.

[278]
MISCELLANEOUS STARTER

Write a song that uses only two different chords. Since the song will be harmonically simple, think about what other elements of the song you could make more interesting to compensate.

Use this starting point or process to build a complete song.

[279]
WORD STARTER

carry

Use this word or phrase in your song's title or part of its lyric, then build a complete song around that.

[280]
CHORD STARTER

C – Em – Dm7 – Gsus4

C major: **I – iii – ii7 – Vsus4**

Write a song that uses this chord progression.

[281]
IDEA STARTER

Write a song for a singer who's afraid of romantic commitment. Think about the specific situation and message. Is the singer going to try to break things off? Will they work harder to deal with their issues?

Use this idea, situation or concept to build a complete song.

[282]
WORD STARTER

viral

Use this word or phrase in your song's title or part of its lyric, then build a complete song around that.

[283]
IDEA STARTER

Write a song about how long it took the singer to find love.
Tell us a little bit about the backstory that led them to find love eventually – and, if you like, whether it happened gradually or suddenly.

Use this idea, situation or concept to build a complete song.

[284]
RHYTHM STARTER

Use this rhythm somewhere in your song's vocal melody, instrumental groove or percussion track.

[285]
WORD STARTER

secrets

Use this word or phrase in your song's title or part of its lyric, then build a complete song around that.

[286]
CHORD STARTER

C – C/B – Am – Dm G

C major: **I – I/7 – vi – ii V**

Write a song that uses this chord progression.

[287]
WORD STARTER

tongue-tied

Use this word or phrase in your song's title or part of its lyric, then build a complete song around that.

[288]
IDEA STARTER

Write a song that says 'This is real love.'

Use this idea, situation or concept to build a complete song.

[289]
MISCELLANEOUS STARTER

Take a four-chord progression from an existing song, run it backwards, then use that progression in your own song. You'll want to be selective about the chords you choose, because some progressions won't sound great in reverse.

Use this starting point or process to build a complete song.

[290]
WORD STARTER

mystic

Use this word or phrase in your song's title or part of its lyric, then build a complete song around that.

[291]
IDEA STARTER

Write a song that says 'I want a real love.' Maybe that message is just in general, or maybe the singer is in a relationship saying that to their significant other.

Use this idea, situation or concept to build a complete song.

[292]
RHYTHM STARTER

Use this rhythm somewhere in your song's vocal melody, instrumental groove or percussion track.

[293]
IDEA STARTER

Write a song that says 'Let's just be friends.' Think about the situation that led up to that message and how the singer feels about it.

Use this idea, situation or concept to build a complete song.

[294]
WORD STARTER

meticulous

Use this word or phrase in your song's title or part of its lyric, then build a complete song around that.

[295]
MISCELLANEOUS STARTER

Take the chord progression (or part of a chord progression) from one of your favorite songs and use it somewhere in a song of your own.

Use this starting point or process to build a complete song.

[296]
IDEA STARTER

Write a song about a temporary love. It could be a summer fling, a one-night stand, a relationship that can't last, anything. Try to make it clear what your singer's attitude is to that relationship.

Use this idea, situation or concept to build a complete song.

[297]
WORD STARTER

labor

Use this word or phrase in your song's title or part of its lyric, then build a complete song around that.

[298]
CHORD STARTER

D – D/F♯ – Em – A7

D major: **I – Ib – ii – V7**

Write a song that uses this chord progression.

[299]
IDEA STARTER

Write a song about an unusual kind of love – any kind that you like. Explain what it is and what's unusual about it. If it's a kind of love that's often misunderstood, you can address that too.

Use this idea, situation or concept to build a complete song.

[300]
WORD STARTER

misbehave

Use this word or phrase in your song's title or part of its lyric, then build a complete song around that.

[301]
RHYTHM STARTER

Use this rhythm somewhere in your song's vocal melody,
instrumental groove or percussion track.

[302]
MISCELLANEOUS STARTER

Write a song that uses only minor chords.

Use this starting point or process to build a complete song.

[303]
WORD STARTER

woo

Use this word or phrase in your song's title or part of its lyric, then build a complete song around that.

[304]
CHORD STARTER

G – Em – F – Dm

G major: **I – vi – ♭VII – v**

Write a song that uses this chord progression.

[305]
IDEA STARTER

Write a song about a major world city – maybe a song about the city itself, something that happened to the singer in the city, or the story of someone else in the city, anything.

Use this idea, situation or concept to build a complete song.

[306]
WORD STARTER

fragile

Use this word or phrase in your song's title or part of its lyric, then build a complete song around that.

[307]
IDEA STARTER

Write a song about a trip to the countryside, somewhere remote or somewhere naturally beautiful.

Use this idea, situation or concept to build a complete song.

[308]
MISCELLANEOUS STARTER

Take a fragment of the vocal melody from an existing song and build your own melody out of it. Try starting with something like four to seven notes.

Use this starting point or process to build a complete song.

[309]
WORD STARTER

labyrinth

Use this word or phrase in your song's title or part of its lyric, then build a complete song around that.

[310]
CHORD STARTER

C – F/C – C – Gsus4

C major: I – IV/1 – I – Vsus4

Write a song that uses this chord progression.

[311]
IDEA STARTER

Write a song about a day at the beach.

Use this idea, situation or concept to build a complete song.

[312]
RHYTHM STARTER

Use this rhythm somewhere in your song's vocal melody,
instrumental groove or percussion track.

[313]
WORD STARTER

sauce

Use this word or phrase in your song's title or part of its lyric, then build a complete song around that.

[314]
CHORD STARTER

Cm – G/B – Cm – G

C minor: **i – Vb – i – V**

Write a song that uses this chord progression.

[315]
WORD STARTER

machine

Use this word or phrase in your song's title or part of its lyric, then build a complete song around that.

[316]
IDEA STARTER

Write a song about someone's home away from home.

Use this idea, situation or concept to build a complete song.

[317]
RHYTHM STARTER

*Use this rhythm somewhere in your song's vocal melody,
instrumental groove or percussion track.*

[318]
WORD STARTER

knock down

*Use this word or phrase in your song's title or part of its lyric, then
build a complete song around that.*

[319]
IDEA STARTER

Write a song about a particular country. Try and focus the song on something physically or culturally interesting about that country.

Use this idea, situation or concept to build a complete song.

[320]
CHORD STARTER

Am – D – Am – E7

A minor: **i – IV – i – V7**

Write a song that uses this chord progression.

[321]
WORD STARTER

forget

Use this word or phrase in your song's title or part of its lyric, then build a complete song around that.

[322]
MISCELLANEOUS STARTER

Take a sample, either vocal or instrumental, from an existing song and incorporate it into a new instrumental groove. Then build a song around that.

Use this starting point or process to build a complete song.

[323]
WORD STARTER

exhausting

Use this word or phrase in your song's title or part of its lyric, then build a complete song around that.

[324]
IDEA STARTER

Write a song about a fictional place.

Use this idea, situation or concept to build a complete song.

[325]
MISCELLANEOUS STARTER

Write a creative cover of one of your favorite songs. Make as many changes as you like, just makes sure the original song stays recognizable.

Use this starting point or process to build a complete song.

[326]
WORD STARTER

perseverance

Use this word or phrase in your song's title or part of its lyric, then build a complete song around that.

[327]
IDEA STARTER

Write a song about somewhere your singer can't go anymore – maybe because it doesn't exist, because they don't have the time or money, or because they're not welcome now.

Use this idea, situation or concept to build a complete song.

[328]
CHORD STARTER

C – G – Am – Am G/B

C major: **I – V – vi – vi Vb**

Write a song that uses this chord progression.

[329]
WORD STARTER

pulse

Use this word or phrase in your song's title or part of its lyric, then build a complete song around that.

[330]
RHYTHM STARTER

Use this rhythm somewhere in your song's vocal melody, instrumental groove or percussion track.

[331]
WORD STARTER

intervention

Use this word or phrase in your song's title or part of its lyric, then build a complete song around that.

[332]
RHYTHM STARTER

Use this rhythm somewhere in your song's vocal melody, instrumental groove or percussion track.

[333]
CHORD STARTER

C – A7 – D7 – G7

C major: **I – VI7 – II7 – V7**

Write a song that uses this chord progression.

[334]
WORD STARTER

swing

Use this word or phrase in your song's title or part of its lyric, then build a complete song around that.

[335]
MISCELLANEOUS STARTER

Write a song that quotes or samples a piece of classical music.
(A lot of classical music is public domain – that is, out of copyright – by now, so you can often do what you like with it.)

Use this starting point or process to build a complete song.

[336]
CHORD STARTER

G – G/B – C – D

G major: **I – Ib – IV – V**

Write a song that uses this chord progression.

[337]
IDEA STARTER

Write a song from a parent to their child. Think about the specific message they want to communicate.

Use this idea, situation or concept to build a complete song.

[338]
WORD STARTER

warrior

Use this word or phrase in your song's title or part of its lyric, then build a complete song around that.

[339]
IDEA STARTER

Write a song from a child to their parent – think about the specific message they want to communicate.

Use this idea, situation or concept to build a complete song.

[340]
MISCELLANEOUS STARTER

Write a song that includes a substantial guitar, keys or sax instrumental somewhere. You might want to write that first and see where it leads you for the rest of the song.

Use this starting point or process to build a complete song.

[341]
WORD STARTER

Washington

Use this word or phrase in your song's title or part of its lyric, then build a complete song around that.

[342]
IDEA STARTER

Write a song from someone to God, or a god. This is a great way to have someone open up about things they might not reveal to another person.

Use this idea, situation or concept to build a complete song.

[343]
RHYTHM STARTER

Use this rhythm somewhere in your song's vocal melody,
instrumental groove or percussion track.

[344]
IDEA STARTER

Write a song to a diary or journal. This is a great way to frame a song sung by someone young or for a young audience.

Use this idea, situation or concept to build a complete song.

[345]
WORD STARTER

ferocious

Use this word or phrase in your song's title or part of its lyric, then build a complete song around that.

[346]
CHORD STARTER

C – C/B – Am – Am/G – F – F/E – Dm – G

C major: **I – I/7 – vi – vi/5 – IV – IV/3 – ii – V**

Write a song that uses this chord progression.

[347]
IDEA STARTER

Write a song about two friends – either from one to the other, a duet between them or a third-person story song about them both.

Use this idea, situation or concept to build a complete song.

[348]
WORD STARTER

heavy

Use this word or phrase in your song's title or part of its lyric, then build a complete song around that.

[349]
MISCELLANEOUS STARTER

Write a song that features an unusual instrument, sound or instrumental technique.

Use this starting point or process to build a complete song.

[350]
RHYTHM STARTER

Use this rhythm somewhere in your song's vocal melody, instrumental groove or percussion track.

[351]
WORD STARTER

hitch

Use this word or phrase in your song's title or part of its lyric, then build a complete song around that.

[352]
CHORD STARTER

C – E♭dim – Dm7 – G7

C major: **I – ♭iii° – ii7 – V7**

Write a song that uses this chord progression.

[353]
IDEA STARTER

Write a song about two enemies – either from one of them to the other, or a third-person story song about both of them.

Use this idea, situation or concept to build a complete song.

[354]
WORD STARTER

sexual

Use this word or phrase in your song's title or part of its lyric, then build a complete song around that.

[355]
IDEA STARTER

Write a song about two former friends or lovers – either from one to the other, a duet between them or a third-person story song about them both.

Use this idea, situation or concept to build a complete song.

[356]
WORD STARTER

inconvenient

Use this word or phrase in your song's title or part of its lyric, then build a complete song around that.

[357]
CHORD STARTER

Em – D – C – B7

E minor: **i – VII – VI – V7**

Write a song that uses this chord progression.

[358]
MISCELLANEOUS STARTER

**Build a percussion track that incorporates unusual sounds –
even real-life sounds you've sampled yourself – then build a
song around that.**

Use this starting point or process to build a complete song.

[359]
WORD STARTER

maybe

Use this word or phrase in your song's title or part of its lyric, then build a complete song around that.

[360]
RHYTHM STARTER

Use this rhythm somewhere in your song's vocal melody, instrumental groove or percussion track.

[361]
IDEA STARTER

Write a song that says 'I can't do this anymore.'

Use this idea, situation or concept to build a complete song.

[362]
WORD STARTER

fusion

Use this word or phrase in your song's title or part of its lyric, then build a complete song around that.

[363]
IDEA STARTER

Write a song that says 'I'll treat you better than he or she does.'

Use this idea, situation or concept to build a complete song.

[364]
CHORD STARTER

C – C7/B♭ – F/A – Fm/A♭

C major: I – I7d – IVb – ivb

Write a song that uses this chord progression.

[365]
WORD STARTER

faint

*Use this word or phrase in your song's title or part of its lyric, then
build a complete song around that.*

[366]
MISCELLANEOUS STARTER

Write a song for just voice and piano or just voice and guitar.
This is a good opportunity to write something that's simple and
intimate.

Use this starting point or process to build a complete song.

[367]
RHYTHM STARTER

Use this rhythm somewhere in your song's vocal melody,
instrumental groove or percussion track.

[368]
WORD STARTER

girlfriend

Use this word or phrase in your song's title or part of its lyric, then
build a complete song around that.

[369]
IDEA STARTER

Write a song that says 'This is who I am. Take it or leave it.'

Use this idea, situation or concept to build a complete song.

[370]
WORD STARTER

guiltless

Use this word or phrase in your song's title or part of its lyric, then build a complete song around that.

[371]
CHORD STARTER

Am – Am/G – F#m7♭5 – F – E – E7/D – Am/C – E7

A minor: **i – i/7 – #vi7♭5 – VI – V – V7d – ic – V7**

Write a song that uses this chord progression.

[372]
RHYTHM STARTER

*Use this rhythm somewhere in your song's vocal melody,
instrumental groove or percussion track.*

[373]
WORD STARTER

call

Use this word or phrase in your song's title or part of its lyric, then build a complete song around that.

[374]
MISCELLANEOUS STARTER

Write a song that's mostly vocals and percussion (or percussion tracks). In other words, use a few pitched instruments or tracks if you like, but keep their importance to a minimum.

Use this starting point or process to build a complete song.

[375]
WORD STARTER

reflection

Use this word or phrase in your song's title or part of its lyric, then build a complete song around that.

[376]
CHORD STARTER

C – C/B – Am – F

C major: I – I/7 – vi – IV

Write a song that uses this chord progression.

[377]
IDEA STARTER

Write a song that says 'You don't get it' or 'You don't understand me.'

Use this idea, situation or concept to build a complete song.

[378]
RHYTHM STARTER

*Use this rhythm somewhere in your song's vocal melody,
instrumental groove or percussion track.*

[379]
IDEA STARTER

Write a confrontation song. Spend some time deciding exactly what the confrontation is about – it could be a dramatic confrontation or a more low-key one – and who is involved.

Use this idea, situation or concept to build a complete song.

[380]
WORD STARTER

imitation

Use this word or phrase in your song's title or part of its lyric, then build a complete song around that.

[381]
RHYTHM STARTER

*Use this rhythm somewhere in your song's vocal melody,
instrumental groove or percussion track.*

[382]
IDEA STARTER

**Write a song about someone struggling to accept
something.** Think about what they're struggling with and
decide whether they ultimately – at least, during the song – can
accept it or not.

Use this idea, situation or concept to build a complete song.

[383]
WORD STARTER

apex

Use this word or phrase in your song's title or part of its lyric, then build a complete song around that.

[384]
MISCELLANEOUS STARTER

Write a song with a vocal range of a sixth or less. That is, write a song that uses a maximum of seven neighboring notes in its vocal part.

Use this starting point or process to build a complete song.

[385]
IDEA STARTER

Write a reconciliation song. Think about what separated two people, why they've been apart so long and now why one (or both) of them wants to reconnect.

Use this idea, situation or concept to build a complete song.

[386]
WORD STARTER

fraternity

Use this word or phrase in your song's title or part of its lyric, then build a complete song around that.

[387]
IDEA STARTER

Write a song about something political – a protest or
message about some kind of injustice, inequality or moral
issue.

Use this idea, situation or concept to build a complete song.

[388]
RHYTHM STARTER

*Use this rhythm somewhere in your song's vocal melody,
instrumental groove or percussion track.*

[389]
WORD STARTER

naked

Use this word or phrase in your song's title or part of its lyric, then build a complete song around that.

[390]
MISCELLANEOUS STARTER

Write a song that uses a modal scale. The Dorian, Mixolydian and Aeolian modes tend to work especially well in songs, but you can use any mode you like.

Use this starting point or process to build a complete song.

[391]
IDEA STARTER

Write a song about human rights – either about a specific group of people and their rights or about people's basic rights more generally.

Use this idea, situation or concept to build a complete song.

[392]
WORD STARTER

out of order

Use this word or phrase in your song's title or part of its lyric, then build a complete song around that.

[393]
IDEA STARTER

Write a song that imagines a better world than this one.
Think about who is going to deliver that message, whether it's you or someone else, and what specifically that person is imagining or advocating for.

Use this idea, situation or concept to build a complete song.

[394]
CHORD STARTER

G – G – C#m7♭5 – C#m7♭5 – C – Am7 – Dsus4 – Dsus4

G major: **I – I – #iv7♭5 – #iv7♭5 – IV – ii7 – Vsus4 – Vsus4**

Write a song that uses this chord progression.

[395]
WORD STARTER

equalize

Use this word or phrase in your song's title or part of its lyric, then build a complete song around that.

[396]
RHYTHM STARTER

Use this rhythm somewhere in your song's vocal melody, instrumental groove or percussion track.

[397]
IDEA STARTER

Write a song about war – maybe a specific war, or just the idea of war in general.

Use this idea, situation or concept to build a complete song.

[398]
WORD STARTER

unleash

Use this word or phrase in your song's title or part of its lyric, then build a complete song around that.

[399]
MISCELLANEOUS STARTER

Write a song that has a chorus in a different but related key to each verse. It might take some effort to make the key transitions, or modulations, work. For bonus points, come up with a song idea and lyric that has a reason for the sections to be in different keys.

Use this starting point or process to build a complete song.

[400]
CHORD STARTER

Am – F7 – D7 – E7

A minor: **i – VI7 – IV7 – V7**

Write a song that uses this chord progression.

[401]
RHYTHM STARTER

Use this rhythm somewhere in your song's vocal melody,
instrumental groove or percussion track.

[402]
IDEA STARTER

Write a song about a real-life event that had (or still has) a
deep significance for you. It could be something you
experienced or witnessed first-hand, or something you heard or
read about.

Use this idea, situation or concept to build a complete song.

[403]
WORD STARTER

world

Use this word or phrase in your song's title or part of its lyric, then build a complete song around that.

[404]
IDEA STARTER

Write a song that says hello – maybe a happy hello, a sad hello, or somewhere in between.

Use this idea, situation or concept to build a complete song.

[405]
CHORD STARTER

C – Gm7 C7 – F – Dm Gsus4

C major: I – v7 I7 – IV – ii Vsus4

Write a song that uses this chord progression.

[406]
RHYTHM STARTER

Use this rhythm somewhere in your song's vocal melody,
instrumental groove or percussion track.

[407]
WORD STARTER

isolation

Use this word or phrase in your song's title or part of its lyric, then build a complete song around that.

[408]
IDEA STARTER

Write a song that says goodbye – maybe a happy goodbye, a sad goodbye, or somewhere in between.

Use this idea, situation or concept to build a complete song.

[409]
MISCELLANEOUS STARTER

Write a perky or energetic melody, then build a song around that. Use the melody anywhere in your song it works, and as your vocal melody or as an instrumental melody as you like.

Use this starting point or process to build a complete song.

[410]
WORD STARTER

morning

Use this word or phrase in your song's title or part of its lyric, then build a complete song around that.

[411]
IDEA STARTER

Write a song that says 'You're beautiful.' Think about how you can talk about someone's physical attractiveness in a way that's specific and fresh.

Use this idea, situation or concept to build a complete song.

[412]
MISCELLANEOUS STARTER

Write an expressive or melancholy melody, then build a song around that. Use the melody anywhere in your song it works, and as your vocal melody or as an instrumental melody as you like.

Use this starting point or process to build a complete song.

[413]
WORD STARTER

maroon

Use this word or phrase in your song's title or part of its lyric, then build a complete song around that.

[414]
CHORD STARTER

C – F/C – Fm/C – C

C major: **I – IV/1 – iv/1 – I**

Write a song that uses this chord progression.

[415]
IDEA STARTER

Write a song that says 'You're beautiful on the inside.' Write a song that's about something deeper than someone's physical attractiveness – what makes them a great, compassionate or generous person.

Use this idea, situation or concept to build a complete song.

[416]
RHYTHM STARTER

Use this rhythm somewhere in your song's vocal melody, instrumental groove or percussion track.

[417]
WORD STARTER

slow

Use this word or phrase in your song's title or part of its lyric, then build a complete song around that.

[418]
IDEA STARTER

Write a song that says 'Thank you.' This could be a song where someone thanks someone for one specific reason or more generally, for a ton of reasons.

Use this idea, situation or concept to build a complete song.

[419]
WORD STARTER

bite

Use this word or phrase in your song's title or part of its lyric, then build a complete song around that.

[420]
IDEA STARTER

Write a song that says 'You're welcome.' Make sure you set up the situation so it's clear who your singer is saying it to and why.

Use this idea, situation or concept to build a complete song.

[421]
RHYTHM STARTER

Use this rhythm somewhere in your song's vocal melody,
instrumental groove or percussion track.

[422]
WORD STARTER

rough edges

Use this word or phrase in your song's title or part of its lyric, then
build a complete song around that.

[423]
MISCELLANEOUS STARTER

Write a detached or conversational melody, then build a song around that. Use the melody anywhere in your song it works, and as your vocal melody or as an instrumental melody as you like.

Use this starting point or process to build a complete song.

[424]
CHORD STARTER

G – B – Em – C

G major: **I – III – vi – IV**

Write a song that uses this chord progression.

[425]
WORD STARTER

joke

Use this word or phrase in your song's title or part of its lyric, then build a complete song around that.

[426]
IDEA STARTER

Write a song that says 'It's gonna be OK' or 'Don't give up.'
It could be a song that delivers a specific message to a specific person or a motivational message to everyone.

Use this idea, situation or concept to build a complete song.

[427]
WORD STARTER

haggle

Use this word or phrase in your song's title or part of its lyric, then build a complete song around that.

[428]
RHYTHM STARTER

Use this rhythm somewhere in your song's vocal melody, instrumental groove or percussion track.

[429]
MISCELLANEOUS STARTER

Write a song whose chorus melody features an octave leap, either up or down.

Use this starting point or process to build a complete song.

[430]
WORD STARTER

picture

Use this word or phrase in your song's title or part of its lyric, then build a complete song around that.

[431]
IDEA STARTER

Write a song that says 'I never meant to hurt you.'

Use this idea, situation or concept to build a complete song.

[432]
CHORD STARTER

C – Am – C – F

C major: I – vi – I – VI

Write a song that uses this chord progression.

[433]
WORD STARTER

lurking

Use this word or phrase in your song's title or part of its lyric, then build a complete song around that.

[434]
RHYTHM STARTER

Use this rhythm somewhere in your song's vocal melody, instrumental groove or percussion track.

[435]
MISCELLANEOUS STARTER

Write a song in C major that never features a plain C major chord. It might include the chord in inversion, with an extension such as a seventh, or with an added note or two.

Use this starting point or process to build a complete song.

[436]
CHORD STARTER

C – E7 – Am – F – Em – Dm – Gsus4 – G

C major: I – III7 – vi – IV – iii – ii – Vsus4 – V

Write a song that uses this chord progression.

[437]
WORD STARTER

eclipse

Use this word or phrase in your song's title or part of its lyric, then build a complete song around that.

[438]
IDEA STARTER

Write a song that says 'We make a great team.'

Use this idea, situation or concept to build a complete song.

[439]
WORD STARTER

one

Use this word or phrase in your song's title or part of its lyric, then build a complete song around that.

[440]
RHYTHM STARTER

Use this rhythm somewhere in your song's vocal melody, instrumental groove or percussion track.

[441]

IDEA STARTER

Write a song that says 'I can't imagine my life without you.'

Use this idea, situation or concept to build a complete song.

[442]

WORD STARTER

mask

Use this word or phrase in your song's title or part of its lyric, then build a complete song around that.

[443]
CHORD STARTER

C – Gsus4 – Am F – C

C major: I – Vsus4 – vi IV – I

Write a song that uses this chord progression.

[444]
IDEA STARTER

Write a song that says 'We're better off together.'

Use this idea, situation or concept to build a complete song.

[445]
MISCELLANEOUS STARTER

Write a song that heavily features a two-note melodic motif. You can repeat and develop the motif or combine it with other melodic motifs as much as you want: just try to include a melody somewhere based on repetitions of a two-note melodic figure.

Use this starting point or process to build a complete song.

[446]
CHORD STARTER

C – A♭ – B♭ – C

C major: **I – ♭VI – ♭VII – I**

Write a song that uses this chord progression.

[447]
WORD STARTER

mixed-up

*Use this word or phrase in your song's title or part of its lyric, then
build a complete song around that.*

[448]
RHYTHM STARTER

*Use this rhythm somewhere in your song's vocal melody,
instrumental groove or percussion track.*

[449]
IDEA STARTER

Write a song that says 'You can trust me' or just 'Trust me.'
Think about why the singer wants the person they're singing to
to trust them, and why that person might be slow to trust them
in this particular situation.

Use this idea, situation or concept to build a complete song.

[450]
WORD STARTER

ecstasy

*Use this word or phrase in your song's title or part of its lyric, then
build a complete song around that.*

[451]

MISCELLANEOUS STARTER

Write a song that heavily features note repetition – one or more melodic motifs that repeat a single note a lot. You could do this as part of a catchy instrumental groove or part of a speech-style vocal melody like, for example, Taylor Swift often writes.

Use this starting point or process to build a complete song.

[452]

IDEA STARTER

Write a song about time – about wasting it, wanting more of it, feeling it pass, anything.

Use this idea, situation or concept to build a complete song.

[453]

WORD STARTER

prowl

Use this word or phrase in your song's title or part of its lyric, then build a complete song around that.

[454]

CHORD STARTER

Am – E – F – C E7/B

A minor: **i – V – VI – III V7c**

Write a song that uses this chord progression.

[455]
WORD STARTER

mouthful

Use this word or phrase in your song's title or part of its lyric, then build a complete song around that.

[456]
IDEA STARTER

Write a song about feeling at home – about why it's so important, why it can be a hard feeling to find, how to feel more at home, anything.

Use this idea, situation or concept to build a complete song.

[457]

MISCELLANEOUS STARTER

Write a song that uses a lot of seventh chords. Any type of seventh will do, depending on what kind of harmonic color you want to give the song. You could also use further extensions – ninths, elevenths and thirteenths – if you like.

Use this starting point or process to build a complete song.

[458]

WORD STARTER

part-time lover

Use this word or phrase in your song's title or part of its lyric, then build a complete song around that.

[459]
CHORD STARTER

C – C – C – Gsus4

C major: I – I – I – Vsus4

Write a song that uses this chord progression.

[460]
RHYTHM STARTER

*Use this rhythm somewhere in your song's vocal melody,
instrumental groove or percussion track.*

[461]
WORD STARTER

lonely

Use this word or phrase in your song's title or part of its lyric, then build a complete song around that.

[462]
IDEA STARTER

Write a song about travel – about somewhere you've been, how it opened your eyes, how to do more of it, why everyone should do it, anything.

Use this idea, situation or concept to build a complete song.

[463]
MISCELLANEOUS STARTER

Write a song that's a guilty pleasure – maybe something simpler or cheesier than you normally write but that aims to be really fun to listen to.

Use this starting point or process to build a complete song.

[464]
WORD STARTER

risky

Use this word or phrase in your song's title or part of its lyric, then build a complete song around that.

[465]
IDEA STARTER

Write a song about emotions – about how to express them more healthily, how to keep them in check, what to do when your head and heart give you different signals, anything.

Use this idea, situation or concept to build a complete song.

[466]
WORD STARTER

Santa Fe

Use this word or phrase in your song's title or part of its lyric, then build a complete song around that.

[467]
IDEA STARTER

Write a song about losing something – your keys, your innocence, your hope for the future, somebody important to you. It's likely to be an emotional song, but try and avoid writing a song that feels too miserable or self-pitying.

Use this idea, situation or concept to build a complete song.

[468]
CHORD STARTER

D – A – B – E

A major: **IV – I – II – V**

Write a song that uses this chord progression.

[469]
WORD STARTER

timeless

Use this word or phrase in your song's title or part of its lyric, then build a complete song around that.

[470]
MISCELLANEOUS STARTER

Write a song that's relaxing or soothing. Try to give it a mood, vibe or message that affects people's moods positively.

Use this starting point or process to build a complete song.

[471]
WORD STARTER

messy

Use this word or phrase in your song's title or part of its lyric, then build a complete song around that.

[472]
CHORD STARTER

Am – D7 – Fm – C

C major: **iv – II7 – iv – I**

Write a song that uses this chord progression.

[473]
IDEA STARTER

Write a song about fashion – about someone who's particularly stylish, why fashion is important or why the way you dress isn't that important, anything.

Use this idea, situation or concept to build a complete song.

[474]
WORD STARTER

independent

Use this word or phrase in your song's title or part of its lyric, then build a complete song around that.

[475]
CHORD STARTER

C – C/E – F – F#dim – C/G – A7 – Dm – G

C major: I – Ib – IV – #iv° – Ic – VI7 – ii – V

Write a song that uses this chord progression.

[476]
IDEA STARTER

Write a song about the power of words – either some particular word or words, or about their power in general.

Use this idea, situation or concept to build a complete song.

[477]
WORD STARTER

make up

*Use this word or phrase in your song's title or part of its lyric, then
build a complete song around that.*

[478]
RHYTHM STARTER

*Use this rhythm somewhere in your song's vocal melody,
instrumental groove or percussion track.*

[479]
IDEA STARTER

Write a song about games – maybe board games, card games, party games, video games or emotional ones.

Use this idea, situation or concept to build a complete song.

[480]
WORD STARTER

astounding

Use this word or phrase in your song's title or part of its lyric, then build a complete song around that.

[481]
CHORD STARTER

C – Dm/C – G/B – G/B

C major: **I – iid – Vb – Vb**

Write a song that uses this chord progression.

[482]
WORD STARTER

self-control

Use this word or phrase in your song's title or part of its lyric, then build a complete song around that.

[483]
IDEA STARTER

Write a song about dreams – either the ones you have at
night or the ones you think about all day.

Use this idea, situation or concept to build a complete song.

[484]
RHYTHM STARTER

Use this rhythm somewhere in your song's vocal melody,
instrumental groove or percussion track.

[485]
WORD STARTER

play

Use this word or phrase in your song's title or part of its lyric, then build a complete song around that.

[486]
IDEA STARTER

Write a song about sex – about why it's fun, not so fun, meaningful, not so meaningful, how to do it, how not to do it, how to talk about it, anything.

Use this idea, situation or concept to build a complete song.

[487]
MISCELLANEOUS STARTER

Write a song about feeling blocked or stuck. Pick any situation you like, but incidentally, this is one great way to bust writer's block: write about it. It always lets you express something specific and personal to help you get writing again.

Use this starting point or process to build a complete song.

[488]
WORD STARTER

poker

Use this word or phrase in your song's title or part of its lyric, then build a complete song around that.

[489]

CHORD STARTER

C – F – B♭ – F

C major: **I – IV – ♭VII – IV**

Write a song that uses this chord progression.

[490]

WORD STARTER

more

Use this word or phrase in your song's title or part of its lyric, then build a complete song around that.

[491]
RHYTHM STARTER

Use this rhythm somewhere in your song's vocal melody,
instrumental groove or percussion track.

[492]
IDEA STARTER

Write a song about anxiety – about someone who is
especially anxious or about anxiety as a condition in general.

Use this idea, situation or concept to build a complete song.

[493]
WORD STARTER

ironic

Use this word or phrase in your song's title or part of its lyric, then build a complete song around that.

[494]
IDEA STARTER

Write a song about fear – about how to overcome it, how it's normal, how it holds people back, anything.

Use this idea, situation or concept to build a complete song.

[495]
MISCELLANEOUS STARTER

Write a song you've thought about writing for ages, but never did. Go ahead – there's always some idea you've been sitting on but waiting for the right time to start. Go for it. That time is now.

Use this starting point or process to build a complete song.

[496]
WORD STARTER

purple

Use this word or phrase in your song's title or part of its lyric, then build a complete song around that.

[497]
IDEA STARTER

Write a song about hope – about how important it is, how to be more hopeful, how to stay positive in adversity, anything.

Use this idea, situation or concept to build a complete song.

[498]
CHORD STARTER

Am – F – Bm7♭5 – E7

A minor: **i – VI – ii7♭5 – V7**

Write a song that uses this chord progression.

[499]
WORD STARTER

someday

Use this word or phrase in your song's title or part of its lyric, then build a complete song around that.

[500]
IDEA STARTER

Write a song about happiness – about how it's important, hard to find, easy to find, undervalued, misunderstood, anything.

Use this idea, situation or concept to build a complete song.

[501]

MISCELLANEOUS STARTER

Write a song that pays homage to one of your favorite songs, songwriters or artists. The song could quote or sample an existing song or just be inspired by it in other ways.

Use this starting point or process to build a complete song.

[CODA]

FEAR OF THE BLANK PAGE – AND HOW TO GET OVER IT

I get it. The blank page – or screen – is scary. And honestly, that fear never completely goes away, no matter how many times you've faced it before.

But the more times you face that fear, the more you understand one important thing: there's no way to avoid it. There's no way round it. In fact, the only way round is through – to get writing.

Yes, blank pages are scary. They could be anything.

But blank pages are also exciting. They could be anything.

Like I've said before, creating songs – or anything – starts with just one 'what if?' that leads to another 'what if?' and then another 'what if?' until you decide the project is done.

Sometimes a 'what if?' leads you straight to an exciting new idea. Sometimes a 'what if?' takes you down a dead end, so you have to back up a little then try a completely different route.

Either way, great.

Either way, you end up with a new, better 'what if?' and one step closer to where you're trying to be.

And the more you lean into the excitement of what your next song could be instead of the fear of what it might – or might not – be, the more fun you'll have and the more interesting songs you'll create.

And the more you lean into making decisive creative choices – even and especially the ones that make you nervous – the sooner you'll be able to make even more decisive creative choices, and the sooner you'll discover what each new song idea could become.

So try things out. See what sticks. Take a chance on a crazy idea and see where it leads. Trust that you'll figure it all out eventually – because you will. You always will.

Focus less on some idea of where your song might or should end up and focus more on the 'what if?' right in front of you. Because, as you know, it'll lead to a new 'what if?' and a new 'what if?' after that.

I wrote this book to give you 501 different kinds of 'what if?' to get you started. They're right in front of you. All you have to do is follow where they take you – and try to enjoy the ride while you do.

* * *

For more ideas on how to be creative and keep writing, I wholeheartedly recommend Steven Pressfield's classic *The War of Art*, as well as Austin Kleon's small but powerful book *Steal Like an Artist*. You'll also find tons of practical advice about creativity and busting writer's block in my book *The Art of Songwriting*.

ALSO BY ED BELL

How to Write a Song (Even If You've Never Written One Before and You Think You Suck)

The definitive, no-nonsense guide to creating new songs from scratch — even if you're a complete beginner.

The Song Foundry 30-Day Challenges

Thirty days of powerful and inspiring songwriting challenges to take your skills to the next level.

The 30-Day Lyric Writing Challenge
The 30-Day Creativity Challenge
The 30-Day Music Writing Challenge
The 30-Day Speed Songwriting Challenge

The Art of Songwriting

A unique and comprehensive songwriting guide, not just about the craft of songwriting but also about how to be more creative, how to make your own rules and how to follow your own path as an artist.

Find out more about all of these titles at **thesongfoundry.com**.

[APPENDIX]

CHORD SYMBOLS QUICK GUIDE

There are a few established ways of using letters, symbols and numbers to notate chords in popular music, as well as their function within the key they're in. So in this Appendix, let's take a moment to clarify exactly which system I've used in this book.

First, I'll explain quickly the seven different chord types you'll find in this book, so you can see how they're represented as both regular chord symbols and in functional (Roman numeral) notation. I've also given you an example of each chord type on a treble-clef staff plus its notes on a keyboard, if you want to brush up on any of that. Each chord is described in words, where the number in brackets indicates the number of half steps (or semitones) the notes are above the chord's root, the lowest note in the chord.

After that, I'll briefly summarize how slash chords – chords where the bass note isn't the chord's root – work and how to interpret the functional chord notation used in this book. That will help you understand how each chord functions within the overall key and will probably come in useful if you decide to transpose any of the chord starters into a different key.

The Seven Chord Types

Major Chord

Chord notation: **C**   Functional notation: **I**

Root, *plus* ***major third*** *above root (4) and* ***perfect fifth*** *above root (7)*

Minor Chord

Chord notation: **Em**   Functional notation: **iii**

Root, *plus* ***minor third*** *above root (3) and* ***perfect fifth*** *above root (7)*

Dominant Seventh (Seventh) Chord

Chord notation: **G7**   Functional notation: **V7**

Root, *plus* ***major third*** *above root (4),* ***perfect fifth*** *above root (7) and* ***minor seventh*** *above root (10)*

Minor Seventh Chord

Chord notation: **Dm7**   Functional notation: **ii7**

Root, *plus **minor third** above root (3)*, ***perfect fifth*** *above root (7) and **minor seventh** above root (10)*

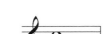 

Suspended Fourth Chord

Chord notation: **Csus4**   Functional notation: **Isus4**

Root, *plus **perfect fourth** above root (5) and **perfect fifth** above root (7)*

Diminished Chord

Chord notation: **Bdim**   Functional notation: **vii°**

Root, *plus **minor third** above root (3) and **diminished fifth** above root (6)*

Minor Seventh Flat Fifth (Half-Diminished) Chord

Chord notation: **F♯m7♭5**   Functional notation: **♯iv7♭5**

Root, *plus **minor third** above root (3),* ***diminished fifth*** *above root (6) and **minor seventh** above root (10)*

Slash Chords

Most of the time, the bass note under a chord is the root of that chord. But it's also possible to put a different note under a chord, to create a so-called 'slash chord', like **C/E** or **Dm/C**.

In each case, the chord name goes before the slash and the bass note goes after the slash – so **C/E** means a C major chord over an E bass, and **Dm/C** means a D minor chord over a C bass.

Functional (Roman Numeral) Notation

The deal with understanding chord progressions is that the chords in themselves don't mean much – what matters is their relationship to the chords around them, and how they fit within the overall key.

This is notated in what's called 'functional notation', using roman numerals that describe the degree of the scale the chord is on. Uppercase numerals represent major chords, lowercase numerals represent minor chords, and all other chords are represented by adding other symbols or letters. (Check the chord types for guidance if you need any.)

So for example, a C major chord in the key of C major is a major chord on the first degree of the scale, so it's chord **I**. In G major, it's the major chord on the fourth degree of the scale, so it's chord **IV**.

A D minor chord in the key of C major is a minor chord on the second degree of the scale, so it's chord **ii**. In G major, it's the minor chord on the fifth degree of the scale, so it's chord **v**.

Slash Chords in Functional Notation

There are two different ways to represent slash chords in functional notation, depending on whether the bass note is in the chord or not.

When the bass note is a note in the chord, the chord is what's called an inverted chord and is notated with a lowercase letter after the chord name, like **iib** or **Ic**.

A 'b' indicates first inversion, where the third of the chord is in the bass – so **iib** in C major means a D minor chord over an F bass, the third of the chord. A 'c' indicates second inversion, where the fifth of the chord is in the bass – so **Ic** in C major is a C major chord over a G bass, the fifth of the chord. And for seventh chords, a 'd' indicates third inversion, where the seventh of the chord is in the bass:

C major:

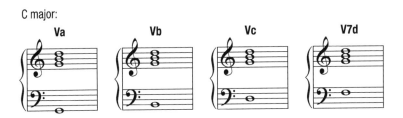

When the bass note *isn't* a note within the chord – often because it's a passing note that connects the bass notes in the two chords on either side – it's notated with the chord's regular functional name, a slash, then the scale degree as an Arabic (regular) number.

So for example, **I/7** indicates chord **I** above the seventh degree of the scale – so **I/7** in C major means a C major chord over a B bass.

For more tools, ideas and inspiration,
visit **thesongfoundry.com**

Made in the USA
Columbia, SC
02 December 2022

72562557R00161